TUSCAN LIVING

First published in the United Kingdom in 2006 by Scriptum Editions
an imprint of Co & Bear Productions (UK) Ltd
Copyright © 2006 Co & Bear Productions (UK) Ltd
Photographs copyright © 2006 Simon McBride

ISBN-10 1–902686–57–8
ISBN-13 978–1–902686–57–8

Publisher Beatrice Vincenzini & Francesco Venturi
Executive Director David Shannon
Design Brian Rust

First edition
1 3 5 7 9 10 8 6 4 2

Printed in Italy

TUSCAN LIVING

SCRIPTUM EDITIONS

TUSCANY HAS BEEN regarded as an earthly paradise; a place of escape and regeneration, of rustic charm and classical culture. Indeed the ancient Romans set a trend for Tuscan country living that has continued almost uninterrupted over the intervening years. Even when the main cities of Florence, Siena, Lucca and Pisa were flourishing through the Renaissance, it was the countryside beyond that beckoned.

In this tranquil setting varied styles of living have evolved over the years, as these pages so vividly reveal. The farmhouse is the most simple form of Tuscan architecture. Originally little more than a bare one or two room dwelling, its thick walls were traditionally built from the field stone lying nearby and its roof covered with handmade terracotta tiles. When the land-holding system was rearranged in the 14th century, many of the farmhouses were vacated by their original peasant farmers and taken over by the middle classes who bought up land with their newfound wealth. They converted the basic farmhouse into a more comfortable place of residence but still retained its earthy quality, reflecting the pastoral traditions of Tuscany.

The same is true of the elegant villas, or palazzi, built by wealthy Tuscans since the 14th and 15th centuries. These beautiful homes combine the artistic sensibilities of the Renaissance with the rustic charm of the countryside. Symmetrical façades and refined detailing around windows and doors are rendered in the local materials of stone, chestnut wood and terracotta. Loggias and terraces open on to pretty gardens replete with fountains and ponds, statues and marble benches.

On an even grander scale are the Baroque Tuscan palazzi with their exquisite frescoed interiors and vast pleasure gardens, or the fortress-villas that have evolved from ancient medieval towers into luxurious country residences. Both types of architecture survive, and now form beautiful homes for their fortunate owners.

In modern times, the inhabitants of Tuscany have brought a new aesthetic to bear on living in this idyllic corner of Italy. Where expensive formal antiques were once sought after, now it is simple farmhouse furniture of oak, chestnut or walnut that is prized. Bare stucco walls, terracotta floor tiles, and ceilings with organic oak beams provide the essential interior backdrop. These rustic textures and forms are combined with touches of contemporary luxury – swimming pools, underfloor heating, large picture windows and soft furnishings designed for lounging and comfort. And in the kitchen,bottles of oil and balsamic vinegar, jars of dried and preserved fruits and vegetables, almond biscuits, wild honey and wine from local vineyard form the basis of daily feasts.

Regardless of architectural style, the country residences of Tuscany share a common feature. They are conceived and arranged with the simple pleasures of rural life in mind: the views of gentle hills terraced with vineyards or orchards, the vistas of winding lanes lined with tall cypress trees; the changing light of the day from spring through winter, and the farming traditions that mark the passing of the seasons. Thus life in Tuscany is a self-contained existence, providing everything the body and spirit could desire.

BLUE-GREEN SHUTTERS and doors punch through the golden hues of the exterior stucco, while climbing roses soften the austere lines of the house. The hill towns of Tuscany (above) are built almost entirely from stone, reflecting their role as safe havens.

SADDLES STAND READY outside the stables of this rustic farmouse ready for a mid-morning ride. Hand-thrown terra-cotta urns planted with geraniums and climbing plants are used to soften the plain stuccoed exterior.

HISTORICALLY, COUNTRY HOUSES were built from whatever materials lay closest to hand; often this meant rough fieldtone that sat close to the surface of the soil. However, the rooftops were covered in terra cotta tiles, in hues of burnt orange and brick red, that provide the archetypal postcard view of Tuscan buildings.

IN NUMEROUS TUSCAN hill towns, cobbled lanes wind past alleys of terraced houses and under the arches of ancient walls. Built from massive blocks of stone, these walls were a crucial fortification in the Middle Ages.

THE STYLE OF this terrace of worker's houses, or *casette a schiera* (opposite) dates back at least to medieval times. The wide door at street level would once have served as the entrance to a workshop, with rooms for living arranged above. The laying of stone for decorative purposes, particularly in mosaic form, was developed by the ancient Romans. Renaissance gardeners perpetuated the passion for patterned stonework with their intricate, pebble-set pavements (below).

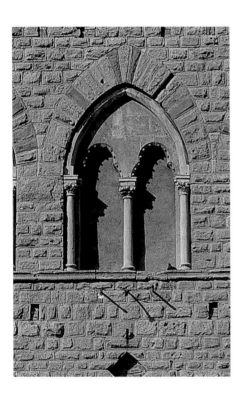

MANY STRUCTURES IN Tuscany are an
archeological jigsaw, constructed from stone and
marble that have been recycled from older
buildings, even Roman ruins.

ROWS OF CYPRESSES and broad gravel paths lead from the house to the garden behind. An iron balustrade, punctutaed by stone pilasters and urns of geraniums, rings a water reserve.

THE GLAZED SHINE of a ceramic jug contrasts with the powdery texture of a terracotta brick wall. Just as the production of Tuscan terracotta developed into a prosperous industry, so too did the making of glazed ceramics, which grew into a fine art. Both products draw on the same high-porosity clays.

20

THE FADED PINKS and golds of the
terracotta pantiles above this simple loggia are
echoed in the terrace paved with terracotta tiles,
the vine-covered brick wall and the fields
beyond. A stone basin (above), affixed to a
garden wall, spills over into a small, still pool
which once would have provided the household
with water for cooking and washing.

TUSCAN ARCHITECTURE THROUGH the ages has demonstrated an imaginative and ingenious range of treatments for doorways. Treatments include edging in stone blocks to blend with the wall; edging with brick or in contrasting stone; stone lintels and pediment; and edging with raised stone blocks.

FRAMED BY TOWERING cypress trees, stands the quintessential stone farmhouse of Tuscany, comprising a tower – possibly dating back to medieval times – with various rooms added on over the years.

DOORS IN TUSCAN houses are characterised by their use of massive wooden panels – and the importance of decorative interest, so much so that no two doors seem alike. They are typically set within a frame of brick or stone, which serves to highlight their position within the façade.

A MAGNIFICENT VAULTED ceiling
constructed from brick gives this living room a
sense of great spaciousness. The texture and
tone of the brick ceiling is repeated in the pale
pink flooring of cotto.

CHILEAN MATÉ POTS, antique leather-bound books, a coffee table made from an 18th-century gilded pedestal, a treasured toy steam engine … The variety of decorative objects to be found in a Tuscan home is as eclectic as its inhabitants.

WOOD-BURNING FIREPLACES heat many homes during the winter months, often using wood cut from nearby forests. As well being functional, the distinctive flues frequently become a central feature of many Tuscan rooms.

THIS CHARMING SCENE conveys Tuscan living at its most gracious, a mix of modern and traditional influences. The fresh apricot colour of the walls is echoed, and even exaggerated, by pretty floral cushions in hues of gold and amber, a fringed orange throw and a small pink lamp.

39

AN ALMOST INFINITE variety of painted finishes, especially in shades of green
and blue, has been applied to wooden elements such as doors, window frames
and shutters. Green and blue are thought to bring a cooling influence in climates
where long hot summers prevail.

LARGE WINDOWS, GLAZED doors,
terracotta paved floors – all give entrance
halls a sense of light and space, as well as
providing virtually uninterrupted views to
the courtyards, or gardens beyond.

THIS EXTRAVAGANT BAROQUE salon, utilises 17th-century paintings, fabrics and *objets d'art* – in soft golds and porcelain pale blues – to complement the richly decorated walls.

NOT ALL INTERIORS are intended for use on a human scale. This antique miniature theatre is one of a number of eighteenth- and nineteenth-century stages that form the prized collection of a theatre patron, each set recreating a scene from an opera.

ALTHOUGH OFTEN FADED with time, bold paint finishes to walls, doors or furniture can bring a dash of vibrant colour to a Tuscan interior.

WHETHER GEOMETRICALLY patterned, or elegantly marbled, ornate table tops provide a striking backdrop for any collection.

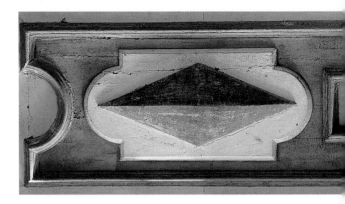

WHETHER STENCILLED OR applied freehand with a brush, decorative effects are commonly found on wooden furniture such as bureaus, dressers and cabinets. The panels of Tuscan pieces lend themselves well to decoration, with floral motifs among the most popular.

THE WALLS ARE kept bare in these magnificent vaulted rooms to show off the texture
and colour of the different wall finishes and to contrast with the furnishings. Plush
crimson upholstery, terracotta floors and large open fireplaces bring warmth to
the austere baronial splendour.

THE CHARACTERISTIC COLOURS
of majolica are embodied in these decorative
plates: white, cobalt blue, antimony yellow
and a ferrous orangey-yellow. Although
inspired by much earlier pottery from Islamic
Mesopatamia, the ceramics known as majolica
originated in Tuscany in the fifteenth century.

THE DELICACY AND beauty of wood decoration in Tuscany dates from the
Renaissance. Natural motifs incorporating leaves and symmetrical patterning have
proved enduring and, with its repeated emblem of a flower-filled urn, this antique
painted cupboard is a more recent example of this tradition.

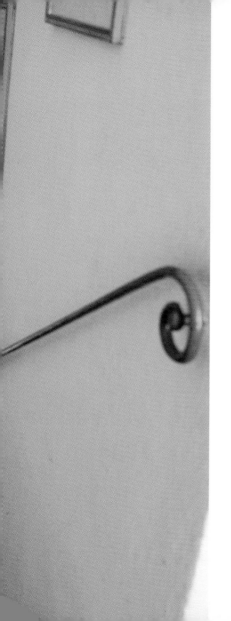

THE ALMOST MONASTIC spartan design and
pale colour scheme of the long staircase (left) is in
stark contrast to the sunny warmth of the bright
yellow hallway (above).

ORNAMENTAL DETAIL is a key part of any Tuscan interior scheme. Even a simple stone staircase takes on a light and elegant appearance with the addition of a decorative balustrade in wrought iron. The balustrade can provide the means for bringing visual interest to an austere backdrop of white-washed walls.

THE LOW BEAMED ceilings, terracotta-paved floors, and a rich sense of colour and texture, give these bedrooms a cosy, rustic feel.

EXUBERANTLY PAINTED
bedheads and wrought-iron
bedsteads, draped in sheer white
fabrics, contrast with the
romantic colours of the walls.

HAND-TINTED PAINTS wash these rooms in blue and yellow, echoed in the ticking of the day bed (above), or the embroidered Arab wedding gown (opposite).

IN BEDROOMS, attention to even
the smallest detail, whether a
porcelain wash basin and jug (above),
or the choice of linens and blankets
enlivening a canopied bed, makes
all the difference.

THE SIMPLICITY, clean lines and clear colours of the pieces in this room perfectly complement the central feature: a magnficent, carved four-poster bed.

THIS VAST BED incorporates bands of rich colour into both the bedstead and the fabrics – a bold design inspired by 18th-century *trompe l'oeil* techinques for rendering marble effects.

THE BEDS are given a sophisticated, yet simple, finish with neutral-coloured canopies, evoking an almost Middle Eastern feel.

DELICATE FRESCOES (opposite) in subdued colours render naturalistic subjects in a romantic style. This form of decoration was very popular during the Renaissance, and it continues to be a typical treatment of earth-toned stucco walls in Tuscany to this day.

THE WARM TONES of antique furnishings mark the living areas and provide the perfect home for copper pots and pans. These are the traditional cooking utensils of Tuscan kitchens, and still a prized domestic accessory.

A REFINED AUSTERITY pervades this tranquil dining room, with its low ceiling and ancient wooden beams. The table and eight matching chairs are cleverly hand-crafted reproductions of nineteenth-century pieces, created in the atelier of Rome-based designer Ilaria Miani. Jars of paint pigment are displayed in a wall niche.

SIMPLE, SCRUBBED WOODEN dressers are staples in the Tuscan kitchen – whether remodelled to accommodate a country-style sink with brass taps, or painted and then rubbed back to create a charming benchtop for cutting freshly baked bread.

THIS KITCHEN is a study in simplicity. Modern
fittings sit unobtrusively under rugged ceiling beams.
hand-made tiles provide the pristine backdrop for
food-themed prints as well as antique copper pots
and pans.

KITCHEN FURNNISHINGS are all of a sturdy, practical nature and of comfortable proportions. Filled with an appealing clutter of saucepans and cooking implements, and scented by dried herbs, the kitchen is the heart of every Tuscan home.

THIS KITCHEN, with its adjoining dining room, would be the focus of household life most of the year, but is a hive of activity during the harvest months when fresh fruit and vegetables can be picked daily from the garden.

A LONG WOODEN table and a large cast-iron stove
dominate this typical farmhouse kitchen. All around the
kitchen, open shelving displays a cheerful clutter of
copper pots and pans and cooking utensils.

THIS BRIGHT and calming kitchen has, as its centrepiece, a large wood-burning stove covered in delicately patterned tiles. Delicious homemade breads and pizzas, often incorporating local produce such as olives, fresh sage and tomatoes, are served around the kitchen table.

THIS MINIMALIST dining room comes to life in the evening when bathed in candle-light from antique candelabra.

THE LONG WOODEN table is the most indispensible piece of furniture in the Tuscan household. It has its origins in bygone days, when the numerous farmworkers sat down together for lunch, often outdoors.

CHAIRS MADE IN Tuscany during the Renaissance depended more on inlay and carving for their decoration than paint effects. From the early 1800s, however, romantic paint effects in pretty colours, often incorporating gilding, became popular throughout Europe.

A SUN-DRENCHED conservatory, with two of the four walls comprising wide arches filled with glazed panes, affords views out into the garden.

THE WARM EARTH tones of terracotta floor tiles and pale golden stucco create a suitably rustic backdrop for a simple wooden bench, weathered clay pots and an antique rack hung with straw sunhats.

INTERIOR WALLS are often covered in stucco, coated with white-wash, or left bare to give a rugged feel to farmhouse hallways.

BOTTLES OF WINE are put down to age in the cool confines of a stone cellar. After bottling, the chesnut wine casks are stacked in the shade, waiting to be cleaned and re-filled with next year's harvest.

AL FRESCO DINING, an important part of tuscan life, is often enjoyed in shady courtyards, amongst flower-laden vines, tubs and vases overflowing with flowers. Paved floors with terracotta tiles and bricks, usually laid in a variety of geometric patterns, have been popoluar since the Roman times.

A SUPERB FEAT of stone engineering, this tunnel vault runs the length of the villa exterior to create a shady arched terrace for dining. The vaulting springs from massive rectangular stone pillars, indicating that the origins of the building may have been a fortress or monastery.

A TUSCAN VILLA wouldn't be complete
without a *loggia*, providing a protected and
private place for eating al fresco, or simply for
admiring the view. This picturesque loggia is set
on a stone floor, under a canopy of vines on
a wooden trellis.

THE PROLIFIC PRODUCTION of terracotta garden pots around Tuscany means that most gardens, no matter how humble, are stocked with a generous supply of basins, pots and urns for planting with herbs, flowers or small fruit trees.

DINNER IS SERVED at a tile-topped table while the sun sets. The magical candlelit atmosphere is enhanced by the wood-burning fireplace, used to grill meats, vegetables and bruschetta – thick slices of country bread dripping with olive oil.

121

JUST AS THE materials of the Tuscan
home closely reflect the immediate
environment, so too the arrangement of
the rooms is designed to harmonise with
nature. Rooms for use in summer, such
as this open-air living area, usually face
north, to give shelter from the sun.

The traditional terracotta tiles of Tuscany, made by hand, are immediately recognisable for their slight unevenness and their colour variation. These tonal differences reflect the mineral content of local clays that have been in use for centuries to make tiles and stucco, to protect and seal external brick walls, and to render interior walls.

Large, irregular slabs of stone make a striking
feature, whether polished in the living area of a
renovated villa (right) – the subtle bands of colour
in the travertine and its relatively fine grain make it
beautifully suited to polishing. – or left in their
natural state in an external courtyard.

THIS TYPICAL VILLA boasts a façade of creamy-beige stucco, symmetrically arranged windows and a doorway edged with pale grey stone; in the garden, pots planted with trees and geraniums and terracotta statues, depicting figures from mythology, complete the idyllic picture. An outdoor stairway of stone, set with a wrought-iron balustrade, is softened with a wash of pale pink on the adjoining walls.

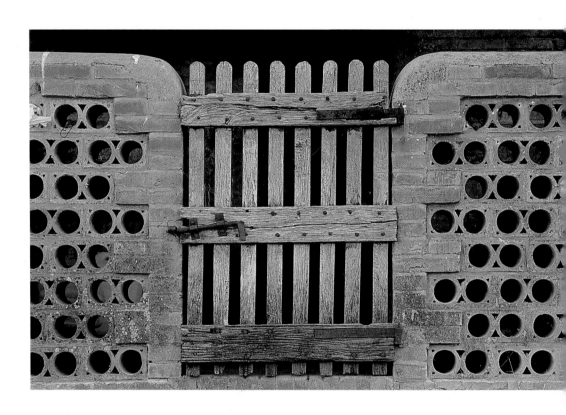

VARIOUS TRADITIONS are displayed here: the rough texture of handmade brick represents the purely functional output of Tuscany's kilns, while the terracotta and stone gargoyles are testament to the sculptural skills of the artisans. Masks like this date from the age of Mannerism and continue to be reproduced today.

SCULPTED TERRACOTTA FINIALS decorate the top of a garden wall surrounding a *limonaia*, or lemon house, at a seventeenth-century villa. The finials are typical of the refined garden designs of Tuscany.

THE REALMS OF FANTASY were explored by Tuscan garden designers and architects of the sixteenth century. Their gardens were populated by exotic creatures and magical, metaphysical elements rendered in stone and marble, creating a visual tension between art and nature. Such ideas have continued to influence garden design.

A FINE EXAMPLE of seventeenth-century Tuscan landscaping and garden design. As was characteristic of the period, water and stone were the dominant elements. Stone was used for constructing everything from staircases and statues to fountains, grottoes and garden seating.

A SIMPLE, TERRACOTTA-EDGED swimming pool is a natural extension of the patio. Its rustic look blends with the rest of the house.

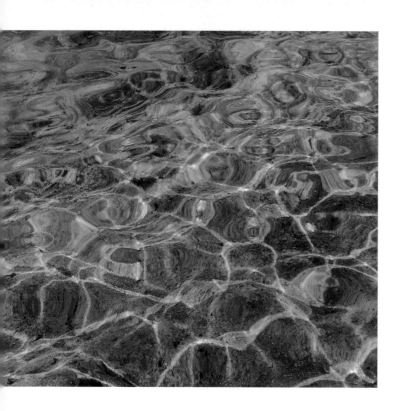

THERE ARE FEW sights more inviting on midsummer Tuscan days
than a shimmering expanse of cool water, edged with sun-warmed
stone and pots of bright pink geraniums, a poolside lounger and a
crisp white canvas sun umbrella.

MOUNTAIN STREAMS spill out into the main Tuscan rivers, which wind their way down through hill towns, valleys and villages on course for the Tyhrrenian Sea. Following on from the legacy left by the ancient Romans, Renaissance architects also built aqueducts, which were often used as a means of feeding the water gardens of Tuscan villas.

151

THE AESTHETIC LEGACY of the Renaissance is evident in even the smallest details of Tuscan civic architecture, in public squares and streets. The humble water faucet is transformed into an object of beauty and imagination, whether in the form of a gryphon, a bird in flight, or a grotesque mask.

THE PUBLIC WATER source was the focal point of village life in Tuscany up until the early twentieth century: an ornamented well at Pienza (above right); a simpler affair at Empoli (left); a washing basin, or *vasce*, with channels to drain the water (above left): and the historic marble well at the village of San Quirico d'Orcia, south of Siena, capped by a streamlined yet graceful wrought-iron arch embellished with swirling brackets.

THE INHABITANTS of Tuscan towns have long been known for their civic pride, reflected in even the most mundane public object. Here, a fixture for tethering horses, attached to a stone wall, the wave-like scroll on the border of a path and the crenellation and crest of a stone basin, are works of art.

WHETHER AN ELEGANT structure of white marble adorned with black iron fixtures, or a much older stone edifice marked with stone columns reminiscent of a temple entrance, the well endures as an important piece of civic architecture, combining a vital public function with great aesthetic expression.

IN WILD CORNERS of many tuscan gardens, crumbling old stone fountains and statuary take on the appearance of primitive, long-forgotten monuments. Exotic creatures rendered in stone and marble create a visual tension between art and nature.

161

THE PLAINEST of water features take on a utilitarian beauty when rendered as simply and unpretentiously as this. The rugged and unsophisticated nature of the wells fits perfectly into the natural environment of a garden.

GLOSSARY

ALABASTER fine-grained type of limestone, white or yellowish white with a translucent appearance. Mined by the Etruscans in Central Italy, and was subsequently used in the Middle Ages, particularly for the tracery of church windows.

ATRIUM an inner courtyard.

BATTISCOPA skirting board edging interior walls, usually made from wood or terracotta.

BRECCIA DI SERAVEZZA deep-violet marble displaying fragments of white, pink and pale green marble, quarried at Stratzema, near Seravezza.

BROCATELLE DE SIENNE dark violet marble with orange spots, quarried at Marmièrecarrarino name given to marble from the quarries of Carrara, in the Apuan Alps.

CASA COLONICA farmhouse, traditional home of the farmer, or agent, managing the landowner's estate. They are typically block-shaped, with a sloping terracotta-tiled roof and dovecote.

CASSEPANCA a long bench with a back and hinged seat that lifted to reveal storage space underneath.

CASSETTE garden box or basin, usually fashioned in terracotta and often featuring relief decoration.

CASETTE A SCHIERE a terrace of small, upright workers' houses, typical of the Tuscan hill towns.

CASSONE wooden storage chest with a hinged lid; one of the most common items of furniture in the Renaissance. Made in three forms: a simple rectangle; convex (boat-shaped); or contoured (like a sarcophagus).

COPPI semi-circular terracotta tile used for roofing.

CORTILE an inner courtyard with arcading.

COTTO terracotta bricks or tiles used for flooring.

CORNICE ornamental moulding that projects along the top of a building, wall or arch, to serve as a finished edge to the structure.

CREDENZA cupboard typical of the Renaissance, characterised by symmetrical placement of drawers and cupboards and architectural-style mouldings. Base was often supported by four carved animal feet.

DANTE one of the main types of chair of the 15th century in Italy. A folding chair featuring X-shaped legs, based on an earlier Roman model.

COLOMBAIA a dovecote.

FRIEZE band that runs below the cornice along an interior wall, usually with a decorated surface; the band that sits between the architrave and the cornice on an exterior wall.

GROTTO an artificial cave, or cavern, decorated with rock and shell work, and typically with water elements and sculptures. First recorded as a feature of ancient Roman gardens and was revived in the Renaissance to become widely used in the Tuscan gardens of grand villas and palazzos.

INTARSIA inlay technique in which shaped three-dimensional pieces of inlay material (usually wood) are set into a hollowed-out space in the ground.

LAVELLO wall-mounted basins with taps, for the garden.

LOGGIA room or gallery that is open to the outdoors on one or more sides.

MAJOLICA (or maiolica) type of tin-glazed earthenware, in which the fired clay is coated with tin glaze to create a white background on which colours can then be applied for decoration, usually blue, yellow, orange, brown and green. The finished surface is shiny and glassy. Majolica is used for tableware, as well as tiles.

MARQUETRY veneer-like inlay technique in which flat pieces of material, such as wood, ivory and shell, are fitted together to create a continuous surface.

MISCHIO DI SERAVEZZA deep-violet marble with clouds of pink, from Seravezza; used widely by the Medici grand dukes for their monuments in Florence during the 16th century.

MOBILI RUSTICI rustic furniture, usually of the 16th, 17th and 18th centuries. Particularly sought-after are wooden chests (*cassepanca*) and Savonarola and Dante chairs.

MONTARENTI marble quarry near Sienna noted for its black-veined marbles.

ORCIO urn, or pitcher with a narrow mouth.

PALAZZO an urban 'palace'; a grand residence.

PENSILE hanging garden, arranged in terraces on a steeply sloping site.

PIETRA FORTE an arenacious limestone traditionally quarried in the hills around Florence.

PIETRA SERENA variety of calcerous, soft grey sandstone found north of Florence on the southern slopes of the Apennines.

PORTICO a roofed entrance to a building that serves as the focal point of the façade; often incorporating columns and a pediment.

QUOINS dressed stone used at the corners of buildings; usually laid with alternating large and small blocks.

SAVONAROLA a folding chair popular in the 15th century. Constructed from a series of interlaced wooden staves, with a low shaped back and armrests, both of which were usually decorated with carving or inlay.

SIENNA BROCATELLO yellowish marble with numerous interlaced veins.

STATUARIO high-quality marble reserved for sculpture.

STUCCO slow-setting plaster used for rendering internal and external walls; primarily made up of gypsum, sand and slaked lime. Developed by the ancient Romans.

TASCA semi-circular terracotta wall containers that are typically ridged or scalloped or festooned with a garland.

TEGOLA a flat terracotta tile used for roofing. In the style developed by the Romans, it is placed directly on the pitched roof structure and then topped with two semi-circular tiles, called *coppi*.

TERRACOTTA from the Italian meaning baked earth, any kind of fired, unglazed pottery. In general usage refers to an object made from a coarse, porous clay that takes on a rich red-gold hue when fired.

TERRA TURCHINA characteristic clay of the pottery town of Impruneta; produces a terracotta that is extremely durable, resistant to frost and temperature changes.

TERRAZZO type of flooring developed by the Romans; marble chips are mixed with concrete and poured into the floor space, then ground and polished to take on a high shine.

TUFA porous grey volcanic stone used for building, particularly by the ancient Romans.

TUSCAN ORDER style of column, as classified by the Roman architect and scholar Vitruvius. One of four types of column; the simplest one, with a smooth, cylindrical shaft – apparently reflecting its origins in the wooden temples of the Etruscans.